88

JOHN FRANCIS CROSS

Here are stories and poems composed in the past couple of years for performance or quiet times, all celebrating life and playing with words to create a place for you to share my wonder and amusement.

CONTENTS

fantastic & bravery

Thanks to Shorai Jones for the phrase
fantastic & bravery

88

If there are 88 days
I will live them.
If there are 88 ways
I *will* find them.
If there are 88 roads
I'll take them.
If there are 88 hands
I'll shake them.
If there are 88 friends
I'll thank them.
If there are 88 fruits
I'll taste them.
If there are 88 lips
YES! I'll *kiss* them.
If there are 88 mysteries
I'll unlock them.
If there are 88 doors I won't knock on them –
I'll choose one,
Walk right in,
Make myself at home
And be myself
Till I'm 88
And I've had my fill
Of these earthly things.
Everything else
Will be my bonus.
And when there are 88 days
I will live them.

Karma

Karma is the law
That whatever you do
Now
Changes your life
Your future
And your future life.
If you smile you *will* be happy
And if you scowl
You'll get permanent lines on your forehead,
Constipation,
A wide birth from amiable strangers
And rebirth as a critically endangered species
Of parasitic head lice
That lives only on the heads
Of partially bald
Red-headed
Chinese women
Over the age of 98.
That doesn't sound fair or balanced, does it?
But, hey, I'm not making the rules.
The rules are made by a woman so wise
No one alive has seen her face.
She created me out of unfired clay,
Paint, human teeth, rock and naked flame.
Nobody knows her name
But I call her *Barbara*.
And Barbara calls me when she wants to tell stories,
Ancient dramas, future scenarios concerning the 62
known moons of Saturn,
And karma happenings
Now.
Such as: The Story of the Woman Who Wears a Mask
to Try to Get Close to the Man She Loves. *The man she*

thinks she loves.
In this mask story there are three characters: a woman, a man and me – I'm kind of neutral.
About me: People say I'm easy to talk to, and normally I start up a conversation with just about anything* by asking something non-invasive and general such as:
What are the common names for horse in your country?
Have you ever had sex with a person named Ermintrude?
Do you know how to pronounce this word:
Սիիթարյան?
And if I want to reap the rewards of influencing people, I sow the seeds of flattery. A sensitive personal observation such as:
'Anyone ever tell you that you smell like summer seaside
toilets?'
I know that's in bad taste and will come back to haunt me but excuse me because I'm having a bad day. I've been arrested for screaming in my own apartment.
[I'm arrested. Go to court. Seven judges sit on my case. Still can't close it. I do tend to over pack.]
It happened like this:

> I go to buy the last loaf of English bread at the bakery but am beaten to it by a queue-jumping five-year-old in a beret. I give up and escape to a bar and get talking to a woman – a mental health advisor, would you believe it? Just my type! And she downs fifteen glasses of draft beer while I amuse her by eating a green paper napkin instead of my salad. Then I invite her back to my place, and she says *yearssh* – which is nice – but

*doors, windows, trees, catfish, men, bamboo, roofs of bike sheds

after she gets there I just can't get rid of her.

That's why I begin to scream. After an hour or so of screaming, the neighbours call the police and when the police come they question the mental health advisor as to her reasons for refusing to leave the apartment, and she explains that for the past twenty-seven years she has been my wife.

But the woman in the *mask story* is infatuated with a man who is a popular playbody. She wants to get close to him and so she lets him fuck her but it doesn't work because he attracts, fucks, then moves on to the next one. And she ends up further away from him than when she started taking her clothes off.

So to get back close to him she puts on a mask and disguises herself as a man. This tactic works and she gets to be one of his gang and soon his solid number-one-buddy and hangs out with him all the time, scheming his conquests, and they get so smooth at it there's no challenge and then he decides he wants to go to a war to prove himself, and he does but gets injured and comes back in very bad shape. She – he – her name is Jimmy now, looks after him very tenderly, while all other buddies fade away because they are phonies but Jimmy's for real. And one day *he*'s better and Jimmy says, mate, let's go on the razz and slay some chicks. And he says, I don't feel the same about all that. And he looks so handsome, vulnerable and wonderfully fuckable lying there when he says it that Jimmy thinks: now is the time! I'm gonna reveal my true identity. And get all naked. And she says, hey, bud, I got a confession to make. And playbody says, same here. He says that in the war his balls were shot off and he no longer has any interest in women or sex, and besides he never had such a good and close relationship as he has with his true pal (that's her, Jimmy) and didn't ever care for any woman as much as he does for his best mate (Jimmy), and without wanting to seem gay or anything, he'd be happy just to hang out with Jim-boy and never set eyes on a woman his whole life.

And Jim says, I gotta take a leak.

And in the toilets she starts crying to Barbara.

And Barbara answers back and because I'm sitting in the next toilet I record the whole thing.

> If you believe the world is good
> Then you'll surely find it is.
> Terrible things are happening every day,
> So much suffering and the pain.
> Yes, I know,
> But I also know that if the base is good
> Then there's still hope to carry on.
> Move in the right way
> And you will live a better day.

Yes, that was the voice of Barbara, Queen of Karma.

Video of Karma performed at Drunk Poets See God, Bar Gari Gari, Tokyo: **youtu.be/SbrCSDL4UQk**

All Lies

All the stories I tell you are lies.
But please realize
Stories are the way we make sense
Of this incomprehensible mess called universe.
I'm taking the path forward.
Come with me.
That way is easier
And with you by my side –
Truer.

Looking Forward To

I'm looking forward to
The Singularity
In the year 2050
When I'll wend up to
Colin, Yuki and Shanti's place
In the foothills of Chichibu,
Far from the station,
Deep in the woods,
With their visions, phobias and prodigy
Already outside the frame
Of mainstream society –
If you stay one night there *you'll never be the same!*
To keep warm they burn the wood
And their place is so a-clutter with goods
It's like living outdoors inside,
Though they do have a cappuccino machine that froths
the top,
And they will say: *Use it anytime,*
Especially round midnight.
But I can never find it.
In any case, theirs is just the base camp
For the ascent to the real place – the Healing Temple,
And at forty-two minutes before dawn
When atmospheric oxygen is at its peak
And birds begin to tweet,
We'll set off for the high hills,
Off grid, no access road, very overgrown, only visible
by spy plane,
But if you live quietly nobody knows if the palace is
occupied
Or what occupies *you* there.
70% of Japan is mountainous
And that's where you find the most powerful herbs

and religious cults –
Though what is a cult except a minor religion you
don't belong to and know nothing about?
How do you enter?
You need stones
And the names of stones:
Chlorite, alabaster, chalcedony.
And make sure in your possession
Are no floor plans of vacant apartments,
Otherwise you will be electrocuted.
And don't touch the microphone.
I just told you! Don't touch the microphone!
On the left side you'll find:
A beautiful Russian-made 19th Century rifle,
Butt inlaid with round silver studs.
And on the right side you'll find a statue of the naked
youth, Harpocrates,
Boy son of Isis,
Said to be the God of secrets and silence,
Based on a misunderstanding of his finger to lip
gesture,
Which is in fact the shape of an ancient Egyptian
hieroglyph meaning:
The only way is up!
You'll sit in the chair with the legs shaped like men's
feet
And if nobody is on the bed –
Which is the only other piece of furniture –
It means you must lie there and be the Master
Of the central breeding station
Of virtual rabbits
Which will be the basis of the future world economy,
The coats and the ear lengths of imaginary bunnies
Subject to sudden folding collapse,
Entailing white-tailed planetary disaster.

So there must be no evidence,
Nothing written down.
Look! There are no words on this page
Nor anywhere in this whole book.
Let me throw it away
And not read but say:
I will show you the way –
Wash your brain,
Dream in the day,
Do nothing – I'll teach you singing.
Do not prioritize any cognitive activities,
In 2050
You and I will be we.
I'm looking forward to it.
Ahhhhh*hhhhhhhh!*
I'm already here.
How can I forget this year?
Of Singularity,
Being healed, focussed and happy.
Now, *be* with me.
You *are* with me.
And that's *my*
Time.
I'm looking forward to.

Image from the website of Ikenoue Bobtail (Café&Fortune)
ikenouebobtail.jimdofree.com/

Tomorrow

Tomorrow,
Oh!
Tomorrow
Is another day
And another way
Of being
I see.
In the future,
When here and now is
Yestereve,
Believe
This:
I will go to the place that shares a cellar
With Bar Gari Gari,
Yes, the Turkish coffee fortune teller.
Have *you* ever been there before?
No?
Thought not.
I will tell you how to get there:
From outside go down the stairs
And come to a fork in the corridor.
(Cutlery is so useful when you want to know the future
more.)
Me, I will take the right turn, go in there and say: I want
to know about tomorrow.
And the fortune-teller will be a gentle person with time
and space to listen and wait for good things to happen,
shawling me in her kind silences.
And she will hand me her name card.
And I will be her only guest.
And I will sit at the counter in the dark brown, study-
like café bar and I will see five saucepans hanging on

the wall, a framed glass picture of the Jägermeister stag with the cross of God between its pagan antlers, a Star of David made of bamboo twigs containing that Jewish icon Kermit the Frog, and a huge poster with the stencilled word

TOʙOЯAMU

which resembles but is not the true

TOMMOROW.

And I will notice all the walls are panelled with gorgeous, long, sinuous planks of wood, edged with bark, the curves of the tree still showing, the wood stained dark, and polished smooth by ages of basement evening fortune-telling.

And the music will be low, rich, ancient and solo. Matching the wood, speaking to the wood, speaking from the wood.

What is this music now flowing, I will ask.

And she will answer, cello suites

I will close my eyes and absorb the cello sounds. The coffee will be good, giving me a lovely feeling holding the warm cup, and as a slight soreness in my throat melts away, I will rest there and relax.

And when the coffee is drunk and cup upended on to the saucer, we will wait the length of two cello movements, then the cup will be exposed again and she will start to see there, in the black grounds, and she will see a person – *me* – energetic, standing big, arms outstretched, accepting and receiving.

And she will foresee an ancestor or a spirit guide or an angel or a goddess, helping me from above, holding a jar of holy healing water, for me, for my spirit, and the fortune-teller will say that I shouldn't make too much effort, I should just accept the nurture, guidance and protection, accept big changes and live on with energy, open and open-hearted, as I am.

She will say: Whatever may have happened to you recently – *has something happened?* she will ask, and seem to weep a little at this point – you will get the support and spirit you need. *Nagare de makaseru* 流れ で 任せる. Go with the flow, leave it to the flow.

This is your big tomorrow.

And I will say, thank you. That's wonderful.

And what about the little tomorrow, the day after today?

And she will say, for that you can choose a card from the word cards.

And the cards will then be arrayed face down before me, so many and so inviting, and I will select the one I want, carefully extracting it from its closest companions. And the word will be:

COMPASSION.

*

Tomorrow never lies!
It rises
From the ash
Of our pasts.
What will be?
Will I be?
Yes, I will
To be
Tomorrow
And now
I take the drug
That takes me

There
Where
I will to tell
You
Yours
And what you'll be
There.
If you will
Volunteer
I'll be the seer.
Give me your hand,
I'll give you to understand,
And will foretell
As I stroke the swell
Of your mound of Venus
And dream us
Together tomorrow,
As I examine the furrows
Lines, twists and turns
I'll see that you burn
With a passion
To be loved.
I will
Let me
Be
Very touching
And say:
I love you
And will love you
For a very long time
Until almost tomorrow.
What happens next
You can't expect
To know
Until

Tomorrow.
Oh!
Tomorrow is another day
And another way
Of being.
I see in the future
That when I arrive at tomorrow I will say: Is this our destination or our destiny?
And now I see its's time for Audience Call and Response.
I'll say: What do we want?
And you'll reply: Tomorrow!
Now we'll try: What do we want?
Tomorrow!
What do we want?
Tomorrow!
When do we want it?
Tomorrow!
You said it. See you there.

Fly Like a Sparrow

I spend most of my life lying down in my apartment
Like a sparrow
That flew top speed into a window pane.
After my last blood check in hospital I cried
Quietly to myself in a waiting room.
And when the nurse injected me with the tubing for a
                                    follow-up CT scan
She hit a nerve (of mine) and yelled, 'Holy shit!'
'For that,' I said (with gritted teeth),
'I should get my arm CT-ed for free.
And now – I want to lie down.'
'You ARE lying down,' she said.
'Besides, you've got two arms –
You only need one to pray.
And anyway, it's stopped raining outside
So you won't need to hold an umbrella.'
But how can I tell her?
'What are you mumbling about?'
How I can I give more bad news to my wife?
And to my mother?
That's what I cried for –
For them
And for myself.
Like a sparrow that flew into a window pane.
Something solid
Nobody was expecting
But they're everywhere.
So I cry
And I lie
And one day I'll fly
Like a sparrow.

Animalistic

If *you* could be an animal,
What would you be?
Human?
I'd be a fox.
A magic white dog-fox,
Coming out of the darkness
And into your life,
With the healing pause.

The image of the magic white dog-fox came to me in a vision.
When the vision was over I said to myself –
Like I guess you would have done, too –
I must make this vision into a T-shirt.
I ordered the T-shirt at the photo communication specialist, *Palette Plaza*, in front of Kitsune station, a local stop on the Odakyu line.
When I went to pick up the T-shirt the staff asked me to confirm the size, colour and design, holding up the T-shirt in front of her face and saying in a low voice: '*If you ever put this shirt on your chest, you will become possessed!*'
'Possessed?'
'Please wash colours separately. *IRASSHAIMASE!*'
Another customer entered the shop.
I cycled home. It was late evening and I was drowsy but I *had* to try on my new T-shirt. I did. Then I dropped into a deep sleep.
I woke with a start in the dark with a foul stench all around me and a soft fat curly lump in my jeans. The stink was myself, and the kinky dump was a tail. I felt bad, good at evil, tricksey, pointy, snappy, tippy-tappy-footed, and hungry-so-hungry for *two-amino-ethane-*

sulfonic-acid.

Two-amino-ethane-sulfonic-acid? What does that mean?

And my voice said:

'*Waowrrrl!* Fox feed! I need. Taurine. From the brain or the eyes or the heart or the blood of dead meat. It's all good – if I killed it, you killed it, or somebody-thing-how killed it. Foxes die without it.'

And I danced outside, down to the river, spending all night on the prowl and the pounce to find:

Two frogs, one toad, an old turtle's head, the pellets of an owl, six slugs, ten snails, a pre-dead pigeon, and the thrown-away remnants of a Korean-style barbecue.

I ate them up quick, vomited sick, and lapped it all up again – because that's what foxes do.

Feeling bad-full of barf I slept till noon and when I awoke the tail was gone and I was human once more.

This nightly fox life dogged me for days and with its heavy protein feed my apartment was reeking making me nauseous until I could bear it no longer.

I went back to Palette Plaza to complain and the staff just smiled and stared at the crotch of my second-hand Levis. I moved my hands to cover the place and felt a bump in my pocket. A note, folded five times, saying: *Go back to 2nd Street*. A buy-and-sell clothing store.

'That's the de-possession chain,' said the staff.

I went back to 2nd Street to sell my black cat shirt and the guy at the counter was a sweet-looking boy who'd been my student when I taught Technical English. He valued my goods, and slipped me eight hundred yen and a campus map of the University of Electro-Communications. There was a red circle in one corner and the figures *22:22*.

That evening, I went to the campus and followed the map to a neglected part of the campus wall, neighbouring the ancient trees, shrine and graveyard, and there I saw a battered wooden shed. The place was deserted and the smell in the air was metallic, electrical and inexplicable. Broken pieces of a crescent moon reflected in puddles in the earth. It was ten twenty-two pm and I was ninety-eight minutes from feeling fucking foxy again.

Inside the hideaway was Saidu, my former post-grad elective student from Mali, looking mysterious in moonlight.

'Mr. Cross, your case *ees* rare *beecorse* you *a'* not *ay* Japanese *minland folks*.'

'I'm not?'

'So there is no point in you praying to the pair of *inari* fox deities at the shrine next door.'

'Oh, I just did.'

'And this is why I mention it. Not a winter-white Hokkaido fox, nor an Arctic fox. You are inhabited by a *pale* fox. They are ranging sub-Saharan from Senegal to Somalia. This is the reason I have been called upon. My people are Dogon. We know the power of the pale fox, good and evil. We have diviners who contact the spirit of pale fox and intercede on our behalf. I can tell you the Who and the How and the Where. But I cannot go with you.'

'Why not?'

'*Beecorse* day and night I am researching the use of AI in the short-sleeved garment industry to get a scholarship and stay in Japan and complete my doctorate.'

'I don't have money to go Dogon land.'

'In this case, there is no hope. Unless – but it is very much unlikely – you have skills of witchcraft or mediumship. Skills you can only get by theft.'

'I know.'

'You know?'

'Yeah, I've been seeing a medium, and pretending to be a normal client, remembering everything he does and stealing it.'

'Mr. Cross, you have a dark side! I should have known this because animal possession only happens to those with an open vein of evil in their innocence face.'

Saidu sighed. 'Animal possession is an epigenetic mechanism. Do you understand?'

'Not 100%'.

'This is the correct answer. To de-possess you need a signal from the sub-conscious mind to start a change in your consciousness. The change restructures your physical body and re-sets its function. De-possession is difficult and even successful de-possession always leaves some animalistic aspect. You may need many perfumes.'

I went home and closed my eyes. In the space there, behind my closed eyes, I used my stolen second sight to see the Dogon village Saidu had named to me, and at the edge of the village, the holy House of Words with the wooden pillars carved with breasts. And I saw the spirit master there, and I put my arm in his, my hand in his, my eyes in his, and together we drew in the sandy dust a grid, and in the grid, shaped circles, mounds and lines of meaning. At dusk we wrote an application: *O Fox, will you leave my body, please?*

We offered warm milk, millet and lizard's blood.

We slept and dreamt and in the night the Fox Spirit came, and made paw prints in the sand for us to interpret and understand. We chanted the prints:

To set me free you need to cry like a fox –
chum titta, chum titta, chuum titta –
With drums and dance and trance –
chum titta, chum titta, chuum titta –

To reach your self:
chum titta, chum titta, chuum titta,
Cry!
Waow-waow waow-waow wow-wow, waaaoow-woaer
waooow!
And at the end of the day
The fox was gone but
I kept
The healing.
I keep the healing.

Solids Dissolve

When I lie in the dark and nothing is shadowy,
When pain is solid and there's no avoiding it,
Sometimes, in hurtful distraction,
I scratch with a pin the surface of my skin
And the flesh below feels the meaning,
Though I never know who writes this poem.
I draw images,
Draw blood,
And colour the pictures
In red,
Imaginary red: fire, warning, desire,
Embers, dangers, vaginas.
Divide by zero,
Nothing is real.
In the cold morning
True warmth is a heart's-breadth from here.
Through the pane
I can't see sunshine,
I'm reading condensation
Instead of books, clouds or sky.
And the drops cry:
All this will pass and the glass become clear,
Drops disappear and tears dry.
And in that time I see
Me, living, pain free
Outside, upright,
Face in sunlight and all else bright
Except
A shadow behind me as reminder
Of the dark and shadow-less place
I will escape
One fine shadowy day
When solids dissolve.

Foreign Lands

I want to go to foreign lands –
Places I've never seen –
Traveling without plans
And losing all my baggage and the way I've been.
I want to lay low
In summer night markets of Guizhou,
Asking: *Yǒu méiyǒu*
Wǒ yào de dōngxī?
And I want to hear sounds
Speaking my soul's history
Voiced by holy choirs in Tbilisi.
I want to slope the high stone streets of Tananarive,
And savour the mélange cuisine
Est-africaine, indonésienne et française.
Malagasy you don't understand?
That's *okeh*, *oueh*, that's good, very *bien*.
And I want to stand
In front of the Indian Ocean,
Feeling warm, charmed and lonesome,
Then kiss someone
With a beautiful face,
Different lips, skin, taste,
Religion and gender,
Whatever
Happens –
Foreign lands.
And my final idea
Is to be foreign and land
In *Bolivia*.

*

I was born by the sea
Named Irish, being English,
Smell of salt coming through the hospital window

From where was a view of a dangerous bay
And a grey, vague distant shore
That my baby-self yearned for,
And has till now.
But that's baby-body, surface journeying,
If my spirit went down from my place of birth
Deep into the earth,
At the far side it would emerge
Foreign and stranded in a sea-less land –
Yes, my spirit would appear
In *Bolivia*.

*

Punk was also born in England.
Sparked by music, firing our lives,
Ashing the past and lighting up our future
That looked so brave
While the flame lasted.
In Bolivia there were only ever ten punks,
And I met three of them.
The first at midnight in a punk club in Amsterdam.
She was a magnetically attractive person in a dog-tooth
suit.
I didn't know she was Bolivian and my first words
were:
Heb je vuur?
(Do you have fire?)
She certainly had.
But I was only an agent
For the reprobate gentleman my housemate
Nicholas James Combe Esq,
Who changed his name, while I knew him, to Arthur
Lager.
We shared an unlettable property above an abandoned
hairdressers on the front line of riot-torn Brixton.
There was a brutal modern view and the name of the

street was *Coldharbour.*

It depressed Arthur that life is never as good as it should be and – worse than that – torments you with signs that it really *could* be.

On days he felt less morose, Arthur would greet me when woke up at noon by singing:

Your pretty face is going to hell!

Hell, hell, hell!

But my 'pretty face' was a reason Arthur Lager associated with me,

Believing it attracted women that he could then make better use of than I.

The Bolivian Punk Goddess was an example of that. She turned out to be a wonderful person, as was her husband, a much older man who owned two larger and more financially rewarding Amsterdam night clubs for which we were guest-listed and felt well out of place.

So we left Amsterdam for other foreign lands.

*

I first met Arthur Lager outside a record shop in Sydney, Australia. He was from Perth, WA, and I was from Northwest England. We exchanged tastes and he introduced me to Suicide – the New York musicians. It was the same night he was my helper in the cheddar-cheese-for-hashish-switch prank. Then I left for China via Manila and we lost touch until one day I saw him outside a record shop in Notting Hill, London. Soon after that we moved to Brixton and had various emotional and artistic adventures together including the Amsterdam mission.

Arthur was a cook, drummer and film-maker – tragically underappreciated. Sample film title: 'Cute Doll (and when I say 'cute doll', I really mean *cute doll*) Falls in the Ocean and is Anally Raped by Plastic Lobsters'. He invited me to be an actor in his films, but only because of the possibility that he then may be able to film my girlfriend, privately.

About seven years later, when my wife first met him, in a shabby London rental, she looked at the literature and art work on display there and said, 'Why are you so much attracted to Black pre-operative male-to-female transsexuals with no clothes on?'

And he said, '*Humph!* Why are *you* attracted to White boys? Such as your husband here, His Holiness Pope Fucking Innocent the First himself!'

At that meeting Arthur Lager told us he'd found his ideal woman, in his words: 'An ugly depressed grouchy heavy-smoking drunkard – *just like me*'.

Dream woman was working in London illegally as a prostitute and got arrested and deported to Angola. Without contact details apart from a 'stage' name, Arthur went to Angola to find her. Sometime later, they did indeed meet. They agreed they were well-matched, got stinking drunk, had a fight and – that was the end of that.

While Arthur was in Angola I was landing foreign in China, Hong Kong, Portugal, India and Japan. We lost touch for ten years until one day I was walking with my wife and a newly-immigrant Canadian friend in Soho, London's red light district, and we came across Arthur with an exotic dancer. The pair of them were handing out flyers for an artistic drum and dance performance, which we all attended.

The last time I saw Arthur was at a retrospective of his films shown on a bitterly cold London Saturday in the basement of a former hospital – for horses. (My friend Vanessa said she recognized my face in the films but I couldn't see it.) Arthur got more and more depressed after that and broke off contact with me, the dancer and everyone else. He sold his shit and escaped to foreign lands.

Less than a year later, in Cambodia, a night porter kicked in the locked door of a room in a hotel for taking whiskey, drugs and whores, and found Arthur Lager alone, on the floor, dead. Cause never known.

But I know we still both live together,

Forever,

In Bolivia.

*

Close your eyes

And look into the dark.

Find the darkest part of the dark.

Look into that dark.

Find the darkest part.

Look.

And see

No thing.

*

My wife I first met in a very foreign city,

In a time and way of life now gone,

In a city where all the streets and buildings we knew

Have been knocked down and built again.

A city made new and unrecognizable.

In that place so long ago and far away

Our first date was for breakfast.

That day I asked her birthday

And she told me March 23rd,

Which is a public holiday

In the only land-locked land on earth

That stops work to celebrate

Dia del Mar –

Ocean Day.

Yes, that's right –

Bolivia.

Since that morning we have been in so many foreign

lands,
That foreign is home
And home foreign.
But that's only baby-body, surface travel.
We've gone deeper, too.
And now find our spirits landed in very foreign places,
See-less, sight-less,
Unsighted, uncharted,
We are in foreign lands beyond
This life and death.
Where from here?
No idea
Except *oblivion*.

*

Audience participation.
Chose a number between 1 and 7.
Choose a colour from the rainbow.
Choose a day.
And a time of day. (Morning, afternoon, evening, night.)
What does it mean?
Your answers mean you are my long lost son, the one
I've never seen, who was taken by his mother at birth.
What's your name?
That was my son's name.
What's your age?
That would be my son's age.
Call me 'Daddy' and slap my palm.
Your mother was a foreigner and so am I, but you are
from here, and always will be.

*

When someone feels unhappy, there are reasons for it.
For example, they're beaten up, don't have money or
are facing death.
But foreign lands have different values. If a person goes
there they'll adopt the values and when the same things

happen they'll feel happy by, for example, being a masochist, loving freedom from cash, or being charmed by the things after death.
Me?
I want to go to the Festival of Camouflage and E.S.P.
But in disguise.
In this poem.
Hidden,
In your mind.
And now
That really is
Foreign Lands.

Some Like it Hot

Imagine
You are hot.
Very *hhhhhhhh*-hot.
Your body begins to melt,
Drop by drop.
You melt into the floor
Drop
By
Drop.
You melt into the earth,
And you are absorbed
Into the dry earth,
Drop
By

Drop.
You spread
And fill the earth,
The entire earth.
And you make the earth moist
And warm.
And the whole earth
Is
you.

*

Now imagine tropical summer nights
Long ago and far away.
A thick mosquito net
Suffocating us
On a on a big bed,
Heavy heat and humidity
Adding to the gravity.
Having showered in so-called cold water

We sat, wet, on the bathroom floor
For as long as it took to dry
By the heat of our naked bodies.
Sex, skin, sweat, limbs.
Exhaustion, distortion of time.
Night is our day and day is night.
Day is dead heat and we've been beaten
By sun, sickening for
Live dark
And the spark
Again
Of lust.
And I am just . . .
And you are just . . .
Enough,
Too much,
Never enough.
It's our hot
Night.
The mosquitos bite,
We are dead
To the world.
It's a dead heat,
But I lose,
You win,
Let's play
Again,
Starting with a kiss,
It will never be better
Than this.
Good God
Amen.

*

You know the facts:
In the past 140 years the average temperature of the

earth has risen by one degree Celsius.

In the past 140 years the average temperature of the human body has dropped by one degree Celsius.

The people with the hottest bodies are poor, and live in poor areas, politically and economically low caste people, eating 'inefficient' foods that instead of being hoarded as body weight, burn inside and turn, wastefully, to heat.

But not everything is bad.

In Belgium, horses are still used for shrimp fishing, pulling nets through the shallows at low tide.

And there are beautiful things to find:

Places, animals, people and moments.

I've seen them.

I see them.

*

Let's see now

A place that doesn't exist anymore,

But did.

Another time, shape, pace

And heat.

Once

Upon a night

From the weight of our bodies in heat

The bed legs broke

BANG!

To go down to the concrete,

I came.

BANG!

That was just once

While every hot night

We dragged chairs outside,

Tilted them back against a wall

And sat, looking up,

Waiting for shooting stars,

For hours.
Necking warm beer,
Bought warm,
In heavy brown bottles,
String-tied together.
Splitting seeds with our teeth,
And spitting husks,
Carelessly,
We talked,
We didn't,
We sat back.
Doing nothing
All night
Long.
Very long.
As long as forever.
Vast and open nights
Of heat,
Insects, frogs,
Silent stars,
And silent us.
Watching for hours
Nothing.
Nothing was ours.
I miss it now.
I weep for it now.
Hot tears.
And salt leaves its trace
On my different face.
This is what was
I celebrate.
No one ever envies the young
Because old is rich and full of *done*.
And the young just maybe come
And then you have nothing,

Like we did
Nothing.
Nothing, nothing, hot nights.
Nowhere now exists.
I exist
Because of you
And the heat.
I cool, am older, but not yet
Cold.

*

To escape the recent heatwave, I applied for a job in a very cool place: a 24/7 convenience store. A temporary pre-fab structure chilled by powerfully globally-warming air conditioners, 2-metre high refrigerators, and deep freezers full of ice-cold goods such as bags of rock ice, ice candies called 'Monika' and ship-side-frozen squid pieces.

I was pleasantly surprised to find that the induction training included an intense series of breathing exercises which calmed me very much until the moment I understood that the target and focus of the meditative practice was the absorption into my soul and being of the 24/7 group of companies' house motto: *Serenity and Cruelty.*

The final stage of the induction process involved standing in a below-zero vault, blindfolded, and wringing the neck of a hot-and-bothered chicken.

I sensed that a serene and cruel and very cool future awaited me.

I stalled.

And I was thrown out, naked, into the street to suffer the heat, to live or die with my ways of anxiety and kindness, and as such, whether I live or not, I will always be
Hot.

19 19 19

It's nineteen years exactly since my dad died,
Today, the 19th day of May
Two thousand and nineteen.
'Time seems to fly by,' says my mum.
Yes, I remember that morning –
How beautiful it was –
The moment I left his bedroom
And body
And went to another room
With a view of trees and sky,
Fresh green leaves, air and dew.
A sparkling world at 6am
Moving on despite him.
Despite not him.
In spite of everything,
Containing everything
Including loss.
How beautiful it was.

Time to Sing

(Oh, has anybody heard
Me sing?
Not yet, not yet.
Let's keep that
My secret.)
There's no time now for anything
Except the MIGHTY WORD,
Which is
No word,
Never word,
A sound,
A colour
I haven't seen yet
But notice
What I'm doing
Is difficult
And awkward as
A Dracula shoe
And you
Are pope-eye blind,
So far away
From seeing
Me
I wonder will I ever be seen
And yet know that
So many others
Have been are will be
Never seen,
Such as the elderly widowed Polish immigrant I met
in Brixton
And whose house was walled with the paintings
Of his wife – skilful – and his own – untutored genius –
Even I recognized,

Me, at the stage of my life I lived as a rock 'n' roll pose,
Absorbed in ever-refined correctness of music,
artefacts and hand-altered clothes,
I saw the thing in the pictures of the man
Who started painting after his wife died to honour her
with the action she did
But outdid her,
That even I saw
And bought four –
Slowly –
Because they were cheap
But I was as poor
As he was.
And I then had to leave the country
And for safe-keeping – ha-ha! –
Lodged the paintings with my sister
Who was in a relationship with somebody in south
London pubs
Which always involved some chaos
And when I came back from Hong Kong
My paintings were gone.
And when I went to the man's house I found he was
dead
And all his paintings had been thrown in a skip.
And there is now no evidence that any single thing ever
existed.
There are no clues
That I wore the Dracula shoes
When the Dutch woman I met in Bretagne
Came to live with me in Fulham,
That she soon left after half sex,
Freaked out by the footwear,
My ex and the disgruntled company I kept
Far apart, close to my heart.
There's no time for all that now,

Nor to explain the 'pope-eye blind' phrase
That came from my first Dutch friend
And which he misheard from a blues record I played
I don't know what when
We shared one room in The Hague
In a time that now seems like
1935 –
Twenty-five years and more before I was even born.
I was just eighteen
And he was such a tall, fucking sexy male nurse and
brawler
My parents thought he was my gay lover.
He wasn't
And complained he could see me walking around naked
from his bus stop
And to stop that!
And I thought – that bus stop's miles away!
I closed the curtains,
All that is gone.
There's no time now for all that lost claustrophobia,
My thousands of notebooks,
Streaming connections –
I need air,
Oxygen
Tank
Of fish
In the sky
By the riverside
With birds in the water
That is flowing, flowing
To calm me, to drown me
With the flowers and the leaves
And the eyes I want to see
Of someone who loves me truly
And takes my hand

And says, 'Johnny, Johnny, It's alright to cry.
It's alright to cry.
Open your heart.
Say, I'm not going to die.
You're going to sing,
There's time to sing –
If you want to sing
Or keep the secrets
Including this one:
There's no need to sing.
There's no need to sing.
Just be.'
Johnny, just be.

Last Minute

If this was my last minute
I'd spend it like Christmas,
Every second a gift.
If this was my last minute
I'd treat it like a tangerine,
Fruity, full of meaning
And very good for me.
If this was my last minute
I'd say *I love you*.
It isn't but I do wonder
How I'd be in it.
Would I be like my friend Katrina
Who felt acceptance in the face of her death
While all around her were panicking?
Katrina survived
By two miracles,
Stopped being an indie rock chick,
Now she's a therapist
With a deep understanding
Of happiness
And impermanence.
If this was my last minute
I'd jump and shake myself like *this!*
If this was my last minute
I'd hug and kiss
The person nearest to me.
I'd roll with it.
Write a poem in it
And ask you for a word to get it going.
If this was my last minute
I'd say *I love you*.
It's not but I do know
Dying is goodbye

And many good things
Begin *bye bye.*
If this was my last minute
I'd understand that dying is separation from living
And that dying is not the greatest tragedy we face.
The greatest tragedy is separation from being
Now, in life,
Existing in a sterile, alien place.
Separated from communication,
Separated from imagining the heart of another,
Separated from human touch,
And separated from the soulful healing
That comes from accepting
A loving hand.
That's the tragedy.
I've known many beautiful people
Who offered me their hand –
And more –
In love.
But *my* hand stayed in its glove.
I always found it hard to open my heart,
This poem is a start.
My *end* has been predicted
But I'm not having it.
Over my dead body!
I say.
Next year?
No fear!
I'm going to be,
Here –
If it's the last thing I do.
If this *was* my last minute
I'd say *I love you.*
It's not
But

I do.

A video of *Last Minute* with music specially created and recorded by Karl is here:

youtu.be/MVRcsq_Phsk

This Poem Exists

This poem exists but
On the page it is like a photograph
Of the poem that first lived
When it came to my mind
By the riverside
With my wife
And 83-year-old neighbour
One Saturday afternoon
After two cups of coffee,
All going to the big game together.
A happy and hopeful moment
That lives
Each time I say it,
The time I wrote it
And if ever you read it.

Promise

In a certain part of Brazil there are meadows – natural meadows – where fireflies occupy hundreds of abandoned termite towers. The termite towers are two metres tall, lumpy tapering cones peppered with tiny holes like windows. And at dusk millions of fireflies pose at the holes, illuminating the meadows with bioluminescent lime-green light, waiting for mates or prey. And all the towers together look like many futuristic cities, bright insect cities, with the promise of love or death.

Near the meadows is a small town where live two middle-aged men, Aurelio and Pedro, who are frustrated with their married sex lives. They try persuading their wives to do a partner swop. They whine, threaten and promise. Eventually and reluctantly the wives agree. Early in the morning after the night before of secret intimacies and new discoveries, Aurelio sits up in bed and says to his new pillow partner, 'It's no good – I just can't sleep for thinking about what the other two are doing!'

'Me, too,' says Pedro.

In fact, the two wives, Fabiana and Bruna, are laughing bitterly.

'Ha! Ha-ha! Eu prometo até que ele morra o porco nunca vai esquecer!'

(But it is easier for me to say it in English.)

'Ha! Ha-ha! I promise until he dies that pig will never forget this!' says Bruna, wife of Aurelio. 'But listen – when you made them promise to go with whoever's keys they picked from the table – how did they get drunk so fast?'

'I put sleeping tablets in their *capeta*,' says Fabiana.

'You beautiful witch! The look on their faces when they

opened their eyes and saw whose keys we had! Haaaa! Ha-haaa!'

'What shall we do now?' says Fabiana.

'I'm going to steal his fucking truck' says Bruna. 'Come with me, Fabiana. It's dawn.'

Bruna drives Fabiana out of town. She says, 'Aurelio never lets me drive his truck. I've hardly ever been out of town. I've never been down this road.'

'Me neither, baby,' says Fabiana. 'Nobody comes out here.'

When the sun is high enough to see everything clearly and there's the promise of a very good day, Bruna stops the truck at the end of a rough road and they start to walk.

They walk through meadows no human being has ever walked through and see the leaves and plants and trees no one has ever seen. They walk past abandonned termite towers, unlit at noon, and they walk beyond noon towards a house, which they approach.

A man comes out of the house and shouts, 'Sisters! Welcome! I was promised you would come but I didn't believe it!'

He's a young, bookish man with a beard and he's not local. He invites them inside and offers sweet fried biscuits and tea. Bruna and Fabiana keep quiet until they have finished them. The man says he's been trying to get workers from an employment agency in the city but they don't turn up, or when they do they go away because of the isolation of the place or the unusual working hours. The man works for EMBRATUR, the Brazilian tourism ministry, and is setting up a guide station for eco-tourists to visit the firefly towers.

'Visitors are coming from Curitiba, Sao Paolo, Florianopolis, even Uraguay, the United States!'

He needs two fit local people to walk with small groups

of tourists around the termite tower meadows each day
at dusk. The pay is good but the work is repetitive and
the place is isolated. Apart from the bearded enthusiast
himself, there's a cook, who is good, and deaf, and the
cook's son who is eight years old and a poet.
Bruna and Fabiana say they will take the work. They
start immediately and are happy to be free and hidden
and financially independent and together. They work
from 3 to 10pm. After a few weeks they send for their
own children, at least those under fifteen. They spend
late mornings and early afternoons walking and
picnicking in the deserted meadows, discovering lovely
secluded spots.
As the poet boy walks with them, he poems.

> There's a promise of spring
> In every breath
> And every step
> I take.
> I'll keep walking
> Through this winter –
> I promise.

I know all this because I stayed there. I spent time with
all of them and walked and picnicked, and I heard their
stories. I went there when I was eighty-eight as I always
promised myself I would.
And the eight-year-old poet took my hand and said:
How do you break a curse?
I want to know, I said.
Make a promise, he said.
I promise you it's true.

Bold Opens!

Men close doors,
Lock with a slam.
I don't want to be a man.
I want to be a coat
And keep warm
By wearing a woman inside me
On winters days
Dark as nights
When I wade on wet pavements
Under heavy skies
And have nowhere to go
Though I go there anyway.
Keeping it simple,
No big words,
My mind can't hold them
Anymore.
Less than before
When
I was super-articulate.
Don't like to think of it.
Just be glad
About what I can do.
But no! And more!
I know
Bold opens!
Doors, windows and ways.
I will think of myself
And others will follow
Wherever,
Whatever
I am.

Tomorrow, too

I will go to a fortune-teller and she will say: What do you hope for, tomorrow?

And I say, I hope to be, myself.

And she says, well, if *you* don't nobody else will.

And she says it with her eyes, not opening her mouth or making a sound, speaking directly to my mind.

And she says, you know the Queen's doctor?

Her Majesty Queen Lizzie of Windsor?

That's the one. And her doctor – the one who lives in a nice shared house in Hackney with a 47-year-old librarian?

I didn't know the Queen of England has more than one doctor.

Yes, she's a lot things wrong with her.

I see.

You will. And this night, when you will be asleep in bed, it will be evening in London, and the Queen's doctor and the librarian will be sitting at a table talking about tomorrow.

And the Queen's doctor will say, 'Do you think I should ride my bicycle to work tomorrow?'

And the librarian will say, 'You know you'll love it. Besides, I won't be able to drive you tomorrow because, as you know, I'll be flying to Alexandria.'

'For a lot of gay sex.'

'For an important librarians' conference with very little time for recreation.'

'You just be careful,' the Queen's doctor will say.

'And it's National Cycle to Work Day!' the librarian will say. 'That combination of publicly endorsed righteousness and intrinsic pleasure will put you in ecstasy the moment you park your pert bot on the bicycle seat tomorrow morning.'

'So, tomorrow's works and pleasures are set,' the Queen's doctor will say with a smile. The librarian will smile, too, and in loving friendship they will clink their wine-filled teacups together.

And tomorrow morning the Queen's doctor will set off, bright and early before the roads are too dusty, and at an intersection on the A104, when the traffic signal is green, that kind of deep oceanic turquoise green that means *GO*, she will go straight ahead, correctly, and be struck side-on, full-force, by a fast-moving, blind-sided, sharp-right-turning truck, and be killed, almost instantly.

And the librarian will not know about this but will feel a disorganizing fret come over him for what reason he'll never be able to explain, and will find himself rushing late for his flight. And he'll get a panicky idea to call Gatwick Airport and tell them there's a bomb on the Emirates 12 to Egypt (via Dubai), calculating, justifiably, that in today's climate of state-engineered fear and efficiency, the call will be taken seriously, quickly investigated, found to be false, and the flight soon re-scheduled and ready to go just about the same time that he will arrive at the boarding gate.

So he calculates and so he acts, and in his calculations the librarian will be correct, except that in his haste and disorder he will omit to imagine the police will be interested in the origin of the bomb-hoax call and because the police have recorded the call without his knowledge or consent, will be able to trace its source to a particular device – a 2-month-old phone – and to a very exact location which, when they seize it, will be the librarian's pocket as he stands at Boarding Gate 38, neat and well-packed for Alexandria encounters. And the police will take both phone and man and will not let go of either for a very long time.

And as for me? I say to the fortune teller.
It's your fortune to know all this, she says.
You will have always known it.
You will always know it.
What does it mean for me? I ask.
It means you are glad to be alive,
Alive and free,
Now, today and, very probably,
Tomorrow.

You Will Understand All This Later

As the dead god said,
The dots connect backwards.
The link between garden gnomes and broken fridges
Is that both are dumped outside
To rot.
And the link between margarine and bus tickets –
Yes! Everything is connected! –
Is that they both taste bad,
At least in my experience.
There is nothing to fear
If we can find the link between me, my happiness
And death.
And all the little pains on the way
And every laugh I've had.
And when it hurts to laugh,
Such as when God breaks my ribs,
I give birth to a *she-she shee!*
And a *he-he hee!*
And a *ha-ha haa!*
Dot, dot, dot . . .

A colourful video using these words is here:
youtu.be/SclhXee7ImU

Side Effects

I cry more,
I laugh more,
I love more,
Lust less.
These are some
Of the side effects.
I walk more,
See more,
Hear more,
Talk more,
Sleep more,
Work less.
These are all my side effects.
Meet friends more,
Made more friends,
Feel loved by family and friends –
Maybe they loved me before but I didn't pay attention,
Accept gifts more gracefully,
Wear self-designed T-shirts,
Have several times reached the monthly threshold of national health insurance medical expenses,
Improved my knowledge of obscure Japanese medical vocabulary,
Own various CD-ROMs showing the inside of my body in 3D form from X-rays, CT scans, MRIs, bone scintigraphy and a biopsy,
Overcame a pathological phobia of hospitals and injections – *well done!*
Now know what it is like to be bald,
Frequently cascade with sweat,
Have two fangs of cancer growing from my backbone that when they bite into my spinal cord, don't let me

forget about it.
These are all side effects.
There's increased vulnerability to infection,
depression, spinal compression, skeletal events,
depletion of blood platelets –
These are all my side effects.
My hair fell out –
Grew back thicker.
I spot more birds, pat more dogs, gather more herbs,
sleep more outdoors, buy fewer clothes.
Mitsu bachi mitsu bachi mitsu bachi bee bee bee I will
be, I will be.
I pray more,
Am drunk less,
God is drunk more,
Drunk Poets See God I cannot always be physically
present there –
It's a sad side effect.
I have fewer regrets except
Perhaps having paid my state pension in full ahead of
time.
I worry less about money
When I'm not earning any.
Draw more, poem more.
With old friends and lovers re-connect – nice side
effect.
Sleep more,
Repeat more –
Fuck – did I say that before?
Anger less,
See there is more,
Feel an ambiguity about my sex,
I'm like a child,
I don't mind.
There is muscle loss, bone thinning, smoother skin,

Difficulties in con- con- con ... er ...
What was that? Oh, I forget –
Maybe it's another side effect.
More self-centred
And yet perhaps more generous.
Some days feel I have the taken on the unwanted cast-off menopause of a weary unkempt middle-aged woman who was until now put upon by her husband, mother, children, boss and bus drivers. She feels much lighter lately, inexplicably.
Chronic pain, acute pain,
Anxiety,
Siestas,
Shocked looks from pharmacists
When they see my prescription
Especially for the tablet that costs 4,500 yen a day.
Compassion,
Companionship,
Love and affection,
Dreams:
I was in the mountains of Iraq with young friends who didn't want to let me go but I had to get away so as not to be late for my sister's wedding, and I got there just in time but it was boring, so me, my sister, my Mum, my Dad (who's been dead nineteen years) and some others got in a big Austin Martin and went for a drive where we got glimpses of stone cities and some kind of Alps, then coming to a charming lane of shops and restaurants I went in one place and said, 'table for fifteen' (not including the dogs and rabbits), and the 'table' was a room of shallow steps which was rotated so that we could get the best view of the southern hills. In a park we played games by throwing tiny latticed spheres made of the most intricately imaginable carved pieces of wood, almost weightless, so that when we

threw them they flattened out, glided, spun, went this way and that, veering crazily to hit the opposing player or come amazingly back to the thrower, or occasionally transforming into huge glowing multi-coloured caterpillar-shaped frameworks that competed with each other to climb the highest nearest available elevated point – a tree, shop, girder – and were able to respond to shouted commands, but only sporadically.
That's what I dreamt last night.
I walk like a crab –
That's a *side* effect.
Dance wildly on one leg
(Though I might have done that anyway, so I'm not sure it's a side effect).
Me and my side effects
Are all messed up.
It's a side effect.
It's a side effect.
Sometimes I feel I am loved by this world.
Sometimes I feel I am loved by this world.

A short movie using these words is here:
youtu.be/OBc6DM37jug

Weeping At Dawn

I'm weeping at dawn
With the dawn
Because of the dawn
In the dawn
Because of its size
Its slowness
Its unstoppable-ness
Its gentleness
Its humanity
All the pain
And kindness
At being alone in it
With everybody else
Alive and dead
[Light seeps in slowly]
Not sad
But weak
Unprotected
Except by dawn
Exposed
Open
Tears releasing strain
Becoming ready
For a day
To be lived
And I the only one
To be
Me
In it
Weeping
For me to be / live
Big
The only day

There is
Alive
A short time
Like everything else
This long dawning
Free
To be helped
And help
{light seeps slowly}

When All Else Has Failed

You think I spend all my time lying down
Listening to Fauré's Requim?
NO!
(Though I have done that.)
I'm dancing
To Soul Power,
Moving in All Directions,
Bug Powder Dust.

I am a poem.
Are you a poem?
I heard you had my ex for breakfast.

I've read so much
But never been anyone else.
I was born this way
And know I'll always stay
And be
One hundred percent me.

If there are fish – just see them.
If there are eggs – just leave them,
There are lovers to break.
Jokes? Just wake them.
Whatever that means.
Seas part. Winds fart. Goats stroke. Wear a cloak.
If there are 88 meanings I think you will see them.
You're so clever and smart it breaks my heart.

Events not captured on CCTV cameras do not exist.

Thousands of people are out there who are conscious

but nobody knows it.
Our innate capacity for forming maps is being eroded
at the neurological level by GPS technology.
So where are we?
In a deep and magnifying silence.

I have that quality where I can go missing for a few
days.
Staring at the sky,
Which has no limit,
It's the entrance to infinity.
It looks blue but isn't;
The blue is an illusion
Caused by refraction
Of sunlight.

Apparently, my first spoken word was _____

Hello! How you doing? How's your leg?
Let me read from the holy Bible:
Book of John, Chapter 14, verse 6:
'I am the way, the truth, and the life.'

I'm gonna wear a head hat,
Eat triangular items.
They say you are what you eat
So you must have eaten one of my friends.
The dog who lives in your mind is thinking of going
somewhere.

If you have no eyes
You can still see.
If you have no feet
I will walk for you.

Patience is a golden road.
Impasse de chanson de ouiseau

Have you noticed it's spider month?
My hands, my hands, the lines on my hands are
changing every day.
They say:
Eat rosemary, drink cold-brewed coffee,
I was happy today.
I say:
Smile inside your mouth.
Smile inside your heart.
Feel yourself on the earth.
You are in a complex world,
Bad things happen and not only in Brasil.
You know about the fight-or-flight responses
But not the third option, and the most common,
Which is to freeze,
Do nothing,
Gift no resistance.
Tonic immobility is involuntary,
Reflexive, physiological.
No way to override this response.
And then you flatter the aggressor
With appeasement behaviour,
Evolutionary gestures
Low-status group members
Use to reduce possibility of violence.
Smiling may save your life,
Or prevent more injury.
Yes, we're genetically programmed
To grin and bear it.

This old woman looks thirty-one
And lives in a frog-shaped house.

She's sick, she says,
Don't tell the trees because they don't need to know
And they might tell the earth.
Doctors and nurses
Are so lonely always
Asking me to come see them.

When all else has failed
Pray to St Jude.
When all else has failed pray to St Jude
And when you see him:
Smile.

Tanaka

I'm fascinated by the forms of ancient Japanese poetry especially the *Tanaka*.

Don't you mean *tanka*?

No, I mean *Tanaka*, a form not widely-used by contemporary poets because of its difficult-to-follow rules such as the content should relate to events that have happened in the past two weeks, and also that there must be an element of surprise.

Here's my *Tanaka One*. And that is the English number 'one', not the Japanese dog sound, '*wan-wan!*'

→ I became suffused with the desire to bring enormous benefits to humanity and be immersed in heroic kinds of volunteer work, perhaps on a vast galactic scale. But remembering the wise advice, 'charity begins at home,' I started by standing on my street corner trying to collect funds – charitable donations, you understand – for myself.

Inexplicably, this didn't go well so I switched my attention towards working for the welfare of a much-loved local institution, the nearest convenience store. And thinking of the sleep-deprived, under-paid workers there, I determined to perpetrate a useful and benign activity that would bring cheer and interest to these workers' infinitely beige and servile lives, all through my own initiative and solitary generosity.

So, at 5:25am last Tuesday, I put on a huge, orange-coloured bicycle poncho, stuck out my arms sideways and burst into the Family Mart convenience store shouting,

'OI! I'M FLYING SQUIRREL MAN!'

But the reception and reaction of the staff was not what I expected.

This is the surprise element of my *Tanaka*.

What happened was that one convenience store staff member turned to the other and said,

'Uh-huh. He's back again. Flying Squirrel Man.'

Completely undaunted by this unforeseen turn of circumstances, I pressed on selflessly with my charitable endeavours.

'Can I order now, please?!' I said.

'Go ahead,' said the staff member.

'Two garlic children!'

'We're out of stock.'

'So when are you getting them in?'

'It's up to the maker,' she said.

'O*Kayyyy* – how about almonds?' I said.

'They're right behind you.'

I picked up a packet and said, 'Do these contain salt? I'm very concerned about my diet.'

She said, 'Sir, what you have in your hand is a packet of boxer briefs.'

'WHAT! That's disgusting! Are they yours?'

'Huh? No! They're a sale item.'

'Right next to the nuts?'

'In the same store, yes, not next to.'

'So where are the almonds?' I cried.

'Hang on. Here you are,' she said.

'Do they contain salt?'

'No, sir.'

'Sugar?'

'No.'

'Lumps of fat?'

'No.'

'Very, very tiny little bacteria-coated monkeys?'

'No.'

'Oh well. I guess I'll just have to comprise and take these. But let me continue with my questioning. MSG?'

'No, sir.'

'Poison?'

'*No!*'

'Bisexual prostitutes?'

'No.'

'Diabetes?'

'No.'

'Astronauts? Puppets? Recently-dead mice? *Hikikomori* software designers? University teachers?'

'No. No. No. No. No.'

'*Air?*'

'Yes, there will be some air in the packet.'

'Nitrogen?'

'Atmospheric nitrogen, yes.'

'Oh, good. Good, good, good. I do like my itsy-bitsy specks of atmospheric nitrogen.'

'Uh-huh.'

'Wait! Were these almonds born in Venezuela?

'No, they're American.'

'American?! I don't want *Americans*! I just want *almonds*! *Wah-wah-wah!* Truly, how *di-ffi-cult* can it be to get almonds for Flying Squirrel Man?'

And I ran from the shop flapping my squirrel wings and weeping tremendously.

And the moral of this *Tanaka* is: If you want to do charity work, avoid nuts.

The Natural World [version 1]

Red!
Is a colour
In The Natural World
At sunset
In the countryside
In Tamil Nadu.
If I were to
Bloody murder you
It would be the time.
Your lips are already red –
Is that because I kissed them?
Or because you want me to kiss them?
And your eyes are blood-red shot.
Is that because we smoked too much hashish?
Or because we stayed up all night
Kissing?
Or have you been crying?
Lack of love and fear of death
Keep us going.
When I die
You *will* cry,
I cry now thinking about that.
But this is not my sunset.
Here I started with red,
Let's go now
To orange
In Morocco.
There's a story in here somewhere.
I think I don't know it and I want to know it.
This is happiness.
Of course there are no stories in The Natural World
Unless we make them

To comfort ourselves
Because lies may hurt but truth is worse.
Will you help me? You will.
Take these seven cards and choose one blind*
With eyes open or closed.
Here goes,
As if by chance,
Although nothing happens by chance
In The Natural World,
*J'aime que la chance joue en ma faveur.***
Here are seven cards,
I take the first card and it is 'dog'.
The dog is looking for a friend. She hasn't any now. She looks at me, I turn a card and it shows 'tree'.
Almost anything can be a murder weapon. But I think in colours. Let's make it an orange tree, named for the fruit. The leaves are green, the bark is brown; it has no fruit now. It is kept alive for an imagined future. Yes, the orange is imaginary while the tree is real. And in the sun-flooded and austere landscape of Morocco, eyes look to trees for information. The dog can't climb the tree but she stands by it because she will see more, hopes to get noticed, or hoping that a friend will come and stand there, too. And in that waiting time I am obliged to take another card.
It is 'sea'.
'I touch the scent', thinks the dog, and starts walking in the direction of the sea scent, not knowing what the sea is but knowing that she wants it. And on her journey there is one more card: 'temperature'.
Day is hot and night is cold. Which is better to walk in? And sleep in? 'I smell the day', thinks the dog, so she

* I wrote 7 words, one each, on 7 cards: *dog, goat, sea, temperature, tree, vehicle, wind.* I put the cards face down and chose cards blindly.
**From *Cool* by Samia Farah 1999

stops and rests daytimes, and at night, when the air is clear in the natural world, she walks on towards the sea.

And before the sea, in the night, by the light of the moon, the land turns yellow. The story moves ahead.

Shuffle 7 cards, take 3.

The cards are: 'tree', 'dog', 'temperature'. That's a repeat; life is often like that.

Dawn comes. A tree provides shelter as the temperature rises throughout the day and the long-journeyed dog rests in tree-made shadows of leaf-shaped green. And green is another colour in our natural world.

The first of the next four cards is: 'dog', again.

The dog stirs as dusk comes. What to do now? On a beach, beneath a tree, where is the friend she sought? She thinks, 'I hear the sweetness,' and I choose a card. 'Tree' again.

The tree is her friend. It has provided good shelter from heat all day and now, at night, it soothes with a scent it exhales from its bark and leaves. A friend can come in many forms.

Another card. 'Wind'.

The wind tells the dog to move along the shore line, so she does, listening and feeling the breeze that is coming from the land and telling the dog and sea of many things.

Fourth card. 'Vehicle'.

You know, I think everything is natural. As trees create leaves, people create hovercrafts, shipping and HGVs; apps and specs. Let us be naturally modern, engaged and married to the world, timeless, too. Now war is over, there is endless anxiety and lack of concentration. In fact there are silent heroes working in private not telling anyone. I wish I could be one of them.

The vehicle takes the dog to another place, she can see the place in the distance and it is blue.

The first card in the blue place is: 'goat'.

And the goat is there in the blue place thinking, 'I see the sound.' And the sound comes nearer. Second card in the blue place: 'temperature.'

The heat increases, the haze rises, the goat is waiting. And now the third card: 'wind'.

Everything changes, the sound is fainter, heat decreases, becomes cold, the goat is tired of waiting and blue becomes indigo – something deeper, another colour in the natural world.

Then we have the card 'vehicle' – it finally arrives, unexpected now and out of place. What card is it carrying? 'Temperature', its own heat, its own world of light and energy in the night. Different rhythms meet. And the next card is: 'wind'. The wind carries the heat and sound of the vehicle here and there like a flame around the place it has stopped in the night. The flame tells of everywhere the vehicle has been and exposes what it contains.

Fourth card: 'dog'.

Of course. The dog hops out of the vehicle and is covered with scents of journey. The dog thinks, 'I taste the love' and blinks in violet white light.

The last three cards. 'Vehicle'.

The vehicle leaves. It has done what was needed here and it goes on to do what is needed elsewhere. This is the life of a vehicle.

Second last card: 'tree'.

This is not the same tree as the first or second tree, but it has many of the same functions. It is also kept alive for an imaginary future, named for what flowers it once had and fruits it may have, but always providing friendly shelter, signposting and something to look at.

And the last card will be: 'goat'.
The goat climbs the tree and eats the leaves.
This the story of The Natural World.
It moves like this.
I'm in there somewhere and so are you.
Between murder and kiss.

The Natural World [LIVE]

I drew 8 captioned pictures, one each, on 8 red cards, and gave them to the audience. Volunteers chose a card, random or not, and I made the story spontaneously based on their choices. The cards were: *almond, blood, coffee, dog, last algorithm, sea, tree, vehicle*. This text is taken word-for-word from a recording made at Drunk Poets See God, Bar Gari Gari, Tokyo, Friday March 29th 2019, by poet Hiroki Kosuge. Words of audience members are in speech marks.

Here are seven cards.*
Please choose one blindly,
With eyes open or closed.
Here goes –
As if by chance,
Although there is no chance
In the Natural World.
J'aime que la chance joue en ma faveur.
Would you like to start?
　'Sure.'
So, choose any card
　'A-ha.'
Either looking or not looking.
　'A-ha. Shall I show you?'
Well, yeah. Otherwise I don't know what it is.
　'Right. I know what I'm doing! I know what I'm doing!'
[Shows: LAST ALGORITHM]
The last algorithm! Oh, that's just a metaphor. There have been metaphors before and there will be metaphors after. It means: the way things work. You know, the point of human existence is survival of the species. And that's very depressing from an individual point of view, and that's why we make stories, which I've already told you but you weren't listening – don't worry, nobody else was – including me. And that also includes that the human species will change and become something else. In the future, the human

species will become the Granddaughter of Google. And when the Granddaughter of Google comes to write the history of the Natural World, I wonder which place it will give to human beings. Of course, the correct space – an organic multicellular organism. And when the Granddaughter of Google meets the algorithm that runs the universe, I wonder will they fucking crash and burn? Whatever happens, *that* is the last algorithm. Natural World – bigger than you think.

'Hm.'

Next card, please.

[Sea]

The Sea!

I went to the sea. And wrote a poem. I felt so free. And the poem is in my back pocket. (*Taking paper from back pocket.*) I say 'poem', it's just a few lines scribbled on a piece of paper. Quite long. (*Unfolding 3-metre-long paper with multi-coloured scribbling.*) It goes like this:

I think in colours,
I hear the sweetness,
I touch the scent,
I see the sound,
I smell the day,
I taste the love,
In the Natural World.

'Hmmmmmmm. I like that one. '

Next card, please.

'Dog!'

Dog! Dog. Inu, inai. I live, I die. The dog doesn't die because it's not alive. It's not a real dog, it's just a picture of a dog. But now, this dog is lodged in your brain beside memories of real dogs, poet readings of dogs, photos of dogs, statues of dogs, possibly poems of dogs, er, dog hairs, hair of the dog, drunk poets see *DOG*. Congratulations you have given birth to a dog! And the dog, er, is going on a journey because she wants to find a friend.

Next card, please.

'Coffee.'

Oh, that's the joker. Congratulations. It just means I will buy you a cup of coffee any time you want.*

Er, next card, please.

'Almond.'

Almond! I'm in thrall to Big Almond. Almonds contain protein, fibre, a lot of minerals such as Vitamin E and magnesium and, er, protein – did I mention that? Almonds that we eat in Japan all come from Central Valley in California. And they're grown in a monoculture which necessitates the destruction of all other plants, trees and flowers in that area, which has decimated the once diverse bee population. But almonds need bees, so every year 30 billion bees are trucked in to the Central Valley to pollinate the, er, almond plants. These are *slave* bees, treated very unnaturally, for example, queens are killed, hives are split in an action called *nuking the hive*. There you have it: Natural World, almonds – good for my skin, bad for bees.

Next card, please.

'Vehicle!'

Yeah, I think everything's natural. Like trees have leaves, we have vehicles, and the dog, erm, goes on a plane, and on the plane she watches a movie and the two actors are pretending to have terminal cancer, and one of them's really rich and drinks this coffee that's the

*The cup of coffee was bought (for Wayne Pounds) at Doutour, Fire Street, Shibuya, 3:30 pm Tuesday 10th April 2019

most expensive coffee in the world, and the other one, who's a fact-checker, finds out that this coffee is made by feeding coffee beans to wild cats, and they shit it out, and that gives the coffee its particular flavor. And when the fact checking one tells the rich one they laugh about this very much until they *cry*. The dog, watching the movie, doesn't laugh, but she does cry.

Another card, please.

'Blood!'

Blood is full of stars and sea. Blood is full of iron and all that iron in blood comes from the stars. And blood carries salt which all comes from the seas. But never try a blood transfusion on your pet dog at home because in fact dogs have 8 types of blood and you could go very wrong. That's our why our dog is running away, his dear friend was killed by a blood transfusion that went wrong at home.

Thank you. Er, is there another card?

'Tree.'

Tree! You know, everything could be a murder weapon. But I think in colours so let's call it an orange tree. It's got, er, green leaves, brown bark, but it hasn't got any oranges on it yet - we call it *orange tree* because we imagine the *future* oranges and it's kept alive for the future imaginary oranges. So, the orange is imaginary but that tree is real.

Thank you. Any more cards?

'I think that's it.'

'I think we got to the end.'

'And that's your time.'

So, er, The Natural World.

It's like that.

It moves like *this*.

I'm in there somewhere, and you are, too.

Between murder and kiss.

Walking

I dreamt I was lying on a table
As I was lying on a table.
In the dream I rolled off,
Became a stray dog,
A fly,
Or some crumbs.
When I woke up
The procedure was done.
I hadn't moved on.
I remember the dream,
Think of dogs, and walking,
And of being free.

Himalayan Orchard

In August 2019 I was Poet-in-Residence at Himalayan Orchard in Himachal Pradesh, India. I also gave poetry workshops at the British Council, Chandigarh and Rukhla primary school, and performed at the first Hobknob arts event in Chandigarh.

I had a wonderful time and it was a deeply meaningful experience.

Huge heartfelt thanks to Michael and Devanshe for inviting me to Himalayan Orchard, for organizing events and for taking such good care of me during my stay.

Thank you to everybody who helped make the journey and Residence possible, especially Mika, also Eiko, Sangenjaya Mama & Papa, Mum and Sarah.

I travelled to India immediately after a 10-day course of External Beam Radiation Therapy at Tokyo Medical Center. Thank you to all staff there.

Thanks to Christina Singh of the British Council, Chandigarh, Anurag Khanna of Hobknob, Chandigarh, and all the pupils and staff of Rukhla primary school.

And thank you to Mr and Mrs Chauhan for welcoming me to their home and treating me with such warmth.

The following five pieces are from those I wrote during my stay, and the first, *Handed to the Hills*, was a birthday gift to Devanshe.

A video of *Handed to the Hills* is here:
youtu.be/OFkriKvlDS8

Handed to the Hills

I was handed up to the hills
By my mother's hands,
By the hands of my sister,
The hands of my wife,
My wife's mother,
My wife's sister,
My friends Michael and Devanshe,
And many others who know me.
And I found the hills calm and still,
And from the very first moment
The hills took me in
And they touched my skin,
Radiating healing
From their trees and their leaves
And their rocks and sky.
And I was allowed to rest
Just like a baby.
And that night as I slept
Rains came
And I awoke refreshed.
And that first morning
Devanshe's mother took me to her temple
Where she anointed the gods
And I too was blessed.
And as I knelt there, calm and still,
I felt so many hands had handed me to the hills,
And that the hills took me in.
I said, 'Thank you everyone',
And I let the healing begin.

What Do I Know?

Before breakfast this morning
I went to stroke the goat
And found the beautiful brown cow had escaped
And got its head stuck in a big blue bucket.
The strong young man called Abhishek
Came and re-tied the cow, gently.
I stroked the goat and asked:
'Do you get milk from this goat?'
Abhishek said, 'No. This is a male goat.'
Then the goat stood up on his hind legs and rammed
my hand with his horns.
And we all three laughed.

Full Moon Night

The moon is crazy bright.
High, small and fierce
In a big dark sky
Which is lording over the hills,
The trees, the earth
And me.
The sky is bigger than everything
But nothing is brighter
Than my full moon tonight.

Missing Word

What is the missing word?
What is the word I seek?
What is the word I need?
When I find it I'll know,
When I find it I'll go ahead
With the rest of my life
With the right person, my wife,
Who told me not to cry,
Who does not believe I'll die,
The one who cares for me the most.
What is the missing word
To say to her
And to myself?
Thanks?
Sorry?
Love?
Time?
Healing?
Happiness?
Am I even listening?
How will I hear it?
Will I read it?
Write it?
Dream it?
Will it come when the pain goes?
When I have energy and ease again?
Is it there on the tip of my ulcerated tongue?
What if I miss it?
It comes and is gone before I can swallow it?
No.
That's not it.
There is no missing word.
Everything is now.

And I have everything.
Nothing is missing.
No need of words
And no more to say.

Jannat*

I stayed nine nights,
Read eight books,
Slept ten hours a day,
And did not feel *bed*-raggled.
Favourite place to stand was the top of the slate steps
Leading from the library to a precipitous

                                           drop.

Favourite place to kneel
Was on the wide cushion before the altar of the family
temple.
Favourite place to lie down
Was on the sofa in the living room,
In kind company.
Favourite thing to do in the morning
Was stroke the goat (and cows).
Yes, I learned the word for heaven,
Was given much buttermilk,
Laughed a lot,
And wandering about
Met a handsome dog called Derek,
A flower called Desdemona
And a nameless cloud.

Jannat = heaven, paradise

Love This

It makes no sense to say:
I love Don Quixote.
Masterpieces like that are public property,
So well-loved by my vilest enemy.
The best I can do
Is give you the fruit
Of my own imagination.
It makes no sense to order in formation
The top ten good books I've ever read.
There are ten better I've never heard of.
And you're going to write one.
Me two,
Eight and ten.

Fantastic & Bravery

I am I have
Fantastic & bravery.
This time, that time, in the now time, in the then time –
Whatever time I need it
To be
To be it.
Not always but mostly
I am
Being / having
Fantastic & bravery.
Enough for when I need it to be
And always thankful for receiving
The gift of
Fantastic & bravery.

Something Slatternly

Explanation of how this piece was made:

Joy Waller said, 'Let's write something with the same first line,' and I said, 'Yes!' So for a day we each looked and listened for likely lines, Joy finding two and me one. We chose one of Joy's – though I also use the other two in my piece. Our chosen line: *There was something slatternly about cooking breakfast in a bathrobe and pyjamas.* We didn't consult on writing until Joy told me she'd finished and was thinking of wearing a bathrobe and pyjamas to perform her piece. I said, I've finished, too, and I'm wearing my bathrobe and pyjamas for sure. We performed the pieces at Drunk Poets See God at Bar Gari Gari, Tokyo, when the theme was *Something Wicked.*

 Drunk Poets See God - John Francis Cross - In His Bathrobe
youtu.be/qVSDyay8Qi8

Drunk Poets See God - Joy Waller - "Portraits of Regret"
youtu.be/sYE38biIqdA

*Joy later told me the line is from *Diary of a Mad Housewife* by Sue Kaufman.

Something Slatternly
[Words of the Petrol Thief and the **Philosopher**]

There was something slatternly about cooking breakfast in a bathrobe and pyjamas. Maybe that's why I loved doing it.

And one day she said:

There's something *slatternly* about cooking in a bathrobe and pyjamas.

If you don't want to live on my good food and fine fortune feel free to leave the kitchen – and starve.

You speak too high and mighty for a self-exiled Mexican petrol thief.

My dear, I'm a petroleum engineer.

On the run from *la policía*.

The powerful make the laws and if power was mine I'd be working for the state oil company. Meanwhile who's to support my mother, five sisters and me?

The gasoline I take comes from beneath my feet

When I stand on my grandfather's land –

Who says I'm a thief?

Mexico is *my* land, stolen by the government,

I siphon small portions from their swag and sell it at prices my people can afford.

Then the government chased me from my land and I landed here,

In your hands.

Why did you run to *Japan*?

I didn't come to a nation, I chose a particular situation and person.

Was that person *me*?

It is now, baby. Here's your hot sauce, beans and coffee.

We ate and drank and later she said:

There *was* something slatternly about your cooking in a bathrobe and pyjamas.

You know, the word *slatternly* is used only for women.

I'm that and I know your real name is *Rose*.

What makes my *Rose* a woman's name?

A rose is beautiful and fragrant.

Am I not?

From deep inside
I feel you are.
And to investigate this feeling
I'm going to press my nose
To every inch of your naked skin.
Now take off the bathrobe and pyjamas
And let me begin.

These aren't pyjamas,
It's an ultra-lightweight flameproof suit.
The dangers of non-state petroleum work
Are fires, explosions and shooting encounters.

Take them off,
I want you unprotected, my prickly Rose.
Lie down and give me truths,
About you and the reasons for all you've done.

My life's story?

No! I'm a goddamn philosopher, not a historian.

Lying in this kitchen I see the corner of the calendar.
It says: *Clocks change Europe, Diwali.*
What does that mean?

It means people now get too fat,
Even in Paris,
Eating to schedules and not to desires.
To follow the wicked ways of clocks
We need alarms,
Tea, coffee
In the morning,
Double espresso for the mannish,
Women pour café au lait,
Cigarrillos all day,
Beer on the way home
Just to settle down
And whiskey before bed
To go blind in the body,
Deaf and numbing it
To the timings of the universe,
Verse of nights, chorus of pains,
Waves of dopamine, high notes of hormones
And the openings of daylight.
From the uncertainties of living
And the chaos of our senses
The same brain events create our thoughts, perceptions and dreams.
Interpretations are all we see,
Everything is not what it seems,
Cooking has other meanings
And one of them is *falsify*.
But there *was* something slatternly about your cooking in a bathrobe.

This is not a bathrobe, it's a baptism garment from the Chinese Christian church in Yokohama.

Are you a *believer*?
I believe in all religions and pray to all the saints.
Especially *El Niño Huachicolero*, the Holy Infant Petrol
Thief, a baby Jesus holding a gasoline can and a
siphoning tube, dressed in white pyjamas.
And I worship your angel face and strange melodic
shape.
It will be Diwali soon.
Festival of Light.
In the darkest night,
On Sunday October 27ᵗʰ.
Let's go away
For three days.
Yes, go away into the tatami room,
Taking every single object out
Except wine and a coffee supply
And staying there,
Lighting a Diwali candle,
Being loose with ourselves,
Making slovenly senses of identity,
Being slatternly
With time
While slow cooking
And taking turns
In the bathrobe.
What will we find?
A word in our minds, the same word.
And we will make our future from it.
Our story?
No! Our philosophy.
And we will make it

Something wicked.

Simultaneous Interpretation = 同時通訳

My favourite colour is black.
いちばん好きな色は白
I have always liked *black*.
好きな色はいつも**白**
Since I was a baby.
昨日の夜から
Black isn't a colour, some people say.
白皆好きですよね
綺麗な色
A-4 の紙、柔らかい豆腐、歯磨き粉、
ホワイトマーカー、人の骨、ぼくの皮膚
Black! Black! Black!
I like black.
The colour of eggs
Gone very bad.
The uncoloured colour.
Sounds like smack, whack,
Knick knack paddy whack
Give a dog a bone.
The bone is white, the dog is black –
I like dogs
Therefore I like black
And dogs
And black dogs especially.
特に白猫、ニャーン
Miaow miaow.
猫は天才
Dogs are loyal.

猫のうんち臭い
Corgi dogs are royal.
I saw the Emperor's dog
And
クレオパトラの猫を見た

もちろん、白

二千年前に死んだ猫
Dead dogs
Are the cause
Of many wars.
That's not true,
うそでしょう

I only said it because
It rhymes.
You see, poetry lies.
横になった

But it doesn't matter
Because I like black.
やっぱり、白

14 Reasons I Know This Rabbit
is 45-years-old and Named Yoshida

1 Mysterionauts told me.

2 It was written on a carrot.

3 It was proved in double-blind experiments with leprechauns.

4 I made a merengue and saw his age and name inside.

5 The number of dots on the rabbit's body divided by the square root of the 45th prime number is 45.

6 I was there at his birth.

7 And the baptism.

8 We are blood brothers.

9 I work in the same company and he sits near me in a cubicle diagonally opposite, so whenever he retrieves dropped dandelion items I see the left side of his left ear.

10 I had a thing with that woman from Personnel, the one with the hearing aid, and she let me have a peek at her databases while she went to the toilet. Now, I don't want to get her any blame (credit) so I should make it clear she didn't actually know I was getting Yoshida's personal details, it's just that she left me standing alone at her workstation while her terminal was unsecured.

11 This information is cut into the palms of my hand.

12 And I am clairvoyant.

13 And good at listening.

14 Especially to rabbits in their mid-40s named Yoshida.

I Used to See a Man

I used to see a man meditating
By the river,
On my way to work.
I was in a hurry,
He was on a bench, usually.
Legs crossed, eyes closed,
Sunburned from being outdoors.
Impassive hard face, clean worn clothes,
Dark.
A bag, similar.
I wondered if he was homeless
And drifting,
A rare bird in this city.
I once saw him in summer
At the public outdoor pool,
Meditating like that.
But the moment I recall most
Is seeing him on the other side
Of the river
Under a big tree,
Inaccessible from the normal path.
How did he get there?
(It's not that difficult.)
And when I saw him there I thought:
Yes!
That tree seeded itself,
A natural act in the middle of the city on a scrap of
                                    wild land,
A natural angle beside the water,
A haven for small birds,
Right by the bank of a slightly deeper part of the flow
Where carp and sometimes catfish
Rest in safe shade.

And he looked apt right there,
Meditating,
Eyes closed, legs crossed,
Upturned hand on each knee,
Very worn into the posture,
Totally at ease.
How did he get there?
I wish I'd spoken to him.
Now I'm not able to hurry
I walk slowly by the river and sometimes
Stop and breathe, eyes closed.
I've even been to the tree.
On the way the Labrador man saw me off path
And shouted: Take care! It's dangerous.
Thank you, I said.
I see now the flow has changed,
It's not the same scene beneath the tree.
I keep looking for him.
But just now I realized
I'm becoming him.
In my own way
I've become him.

Today

Photo of a Mexican church.
Yellow and red lilies, tall
By a sluggish river.
A shady leafy area with natural spring water
On a hot day.
A café cool and quiet to rest.
Shared anger and dislike
Of a mutual acquaintance:
'Oh, I've already punched his face in,' said my friend,
'In my mind, very thoroughly.'
Scent of pimento, freshly picked.
Strange cries of herons
Flying overhead awkwardly.
Musing on the thoughts of a motionless heron, stand
ing tall by the river's edge –
Aware but not anxious,
Acting naturally, like people once did.
Gentle breeze on my cheek.
Taste of the bread I made myself.
And all this my life
Today.

Beautiful Day

Beautiful day
And beautiful pain.
Everything has a cost
And I am happy to pay
For the whole day
Including my pain,
With my pain.
The same again tomorrow
And again and again,
Paying my way
For other days like this,
Of beauty and cost.
This is my lot.

Howl: What's Happening to Me

I want to say or write what's really happening to me
So at the bar I tell Frank Spignese:
'Two years ago I was diagnosed with terminal cancer.'
He says, 'Yeah, man, I heard it from Anna.
But like most Anna stories it's hard to believe.'
Then follows with a tale about his battle with obesity –
Including the numbers: 100, 80 and 83 –
But I can't catch what's his fat fact now.
So I say, 'I also dropped some kilos.'
But refrain from saying, 'to below 53'.
And when he offers a drink to me
To go with his two gin tonics,
I say, 'Thanks, but I'll stick to the complementary
tomato juice.'
(What with all that's happened to me.
With all the wonder and laughs
Such as reading of a teenage girl tickling her clitoris
With long cool ladylike fingers
To a glossy shot of a handsome movie idol
In a slim volume loaned to me
By an intriguing younger female.
Understanding how erotic it is
But not feeling it,
Grieving for that lost lust,
For one gasp-long pang,
Then *back*
To being alive
As a happy child,
Second time,
Aware of the first
And everything else,
Not fearing death
Only dying

And leaving behind grieving people
Who deserve much better.
And I remember
The last thing my Dad said to me before he died:
Images come into my mind
But not necessarily the ones I want.
And now I know how he was
When I wake up heart-thumped and feverish from
dreams
Of losing my wife in a frightening new city
Where I'm working undercover and unable to tell her,
And am the outcast victim of misplaced social stigma
Created by small boys and my mother,
And am the video director of humiliating sex,
With unspeakable torture waiting just round the
corner,
And also – a lovely cuddly bunny.
It almost sounds funny
And it must be
Because I for one now laugh:
Ha-ha!
There is no going back,
No unseeing
Images I've dreamed
And that rack my nights till dawns.
In a brief pause
Between two forms
Of chemical castration,
I experience spontaneous ejaculation
And the semen is coagulated claret,
Melted blood sausage,
From two-year-old wounds
Come from the biopsy
When the young doctor snipped
Holding a long biter-stick

Up my arse
To clip parts of my prostate tumour.
I feel him from behind inject me with anaesthetic and immediately begin.
Then hear a nurse whisper to him:
Doctor, shouldn't we wait five or ten minutes for the patient's numbness to set in?
While another nurse holds my hand
Or rubs my feet
That are icy cold
From fear,
My body saying: this is no dream, it's real
And happening
To me.
I'm not sleeping now and have no regrets
That I'm alive and aware in every sense,
Turning my face up to the sun.
And so I go on,
Now in the twenty-seventh month of the same fatal disease that killed my Dad
Twenty-seven months after his own life-changing diagnosis.
Changed in so many ways,
I've become the acceptor of gifts,
The love of strangers and friends –
And I tell them
I went through three levels of security,
Giving proof of my identity
In Japanese,
Was injected with radioactive material
And made to wait in a sealed windowless basement vault
Until a hospital technician clumped in to scan me,
Him wearing a protective suit and masked so I couldn't see his features

But my face was exposed, and he asked me, in Japanese,
'Do you speak Japanese?'
And I answered, in Japanese,
'No, not a word, I only speak French.'
'French?'
'Yeah, I was told all Tokyo radiation technicians speak French.'
He said, '*Eyyy?* I don't know what to do next! Only French?'
'Yeah, French.'
In Japanese.
This went on for several minutes.
Sounds funny
And it would be
If it wasn't me
Really in it.
Now
People who know my diet but not the reasons for it
Say: 'Good on you, mate. I respect you, keeping yourself pure.'
Meaning nothing of the sort, believing I'm a precious stuck-up kill-joy,
When the opposite is true – I'm living for joy, looking for joy,
But without the wild frenzy I burned when younger,
When I was so reckless even my depressed heroin-taking rock-band-drummer housemate warned me,
'*Go easy, John. Don't do it.*'
And that was just at the moment I was going to snort a line each of salt and pepper as a dare for ten bucks or some intoxicating hit,
Spin,
Thrill.
Now I'm wild like an animal
Let loose from sense of good and evil.

The only 'good' is being fully alive, fully aware,
With no evil intentions ever.
Chemo gave me fever,
Ear sharp pain for days,
Skin covered in red welts,
Muscle pain, joint pain,
Constipation, diarrhoea, nausea,
Floating turd thoughts of death and dying,
Exhaustion, insomnia –
You can read all this kind of stuff on Wikipedia –
And I was ready to continue
But the hospital refused me
Saying, 'The next shot may kill you.
We'd have the liability,
Might even get sued.'
But that's just glamourous dark drama,
The thing that's really hard
Is each step every day,
Continuing this way
In isolation,
With no confidence,
Withering under minor criticism
And symptoms,
Out of my control.
My wife is a sharp spark to me,
And I am charged
With being
Positive,
And I am
Truly –
If I wasn't,
If it was a lie,
I would die.
I don't want to die.
I will be always alive.

I'm not fooling
Myself
But may be fooling you
(No single word is true).
And this winter morning at 8 am
I stand in front of the sun,
Close my eyes,
Breathe in
Red and the orange and the yellow and pink.
I'm living
And laughing,
And opening my eyes,
Wild
Baby animal,
And I see
This is what's happening to me.)
And I howl.
Yes!!!

Carlos is Us

PART ONE

Carlos Ghosn escaped Japan
In a musical instrument case.
Who's instrument?
What instrument?
Where's that instrument now?
How is it being carried around?
Carlos Ghosn is 169 cm tall, weighs 78 kilos and his
body measurements are 107 cm, 89 cm and 94 cm.
How could he fit in a double bass case?
(Which may be 200 cm tall but squeezes 22 cm at the
narrowest point.)

PART TWO

Carlos was fleeing from justice and injustice,
Wanted pre-trial freedom,
Had a quarrel with the system,
Didn't want to be treated the same way as everybody
else living in this country.
And I completely understand him.
I want special treatment for me, too.
I want mitochondrial biogenesis,
Enhanced autophagy,
Indolent disease progression,
And / or miracles.
Is my poetry just listy?
Fuck, yeah!
Way better than listless.
Listy means *active*, *eager* and *involved*.
Sure I am
Listy lusty left-field funky,

Stand on left leg for 169 seconds
Blindly,
Well-
Balanced,
Angry when correctly
So,
Sew
My own curtain,
Far from curtains,
Up not down,
I'm standing,
Getting into no black box,
Sticking in Japan.
I love Tokyo's winter sun,
Sky, stars, moon and clouds.
I lay in the dark
On typhoon-flood-carried sand
At Tama River's wildest part,
At night.
Flood debris hanging five metres above me
And infinitely
Above me
Orion
Through the black-twigged trees,
Like Christmas illuminations
Dotted on branches.
A kind of madness
If you saw me
Calmly counting breathing
Flat out
In the night,
Very here,
Not escaping,
Not in a box
Going to Turkey

Just after Christmas
In the season
Of clear skies
(Private planes)
And slight frosts.
I love walking incognito
To the 80 yen Family Mart coffee
Before 7 am
With dawn sun
Doubled in the water
Of the little river –
No River –
By my soviet-style apartment,
Very old, 1960s,
Just like me.
Fifth floor equals penthouse,
Many stair steps,
View of Fuji,
Sprinkled powder
Snow on the mountains,
Before it
I'm making pizza,
Chapattis,
In my oven toaster.
We
Grow broccoli,
Spinach, baby radish, Italian parsley,
Edible chrysanthemum,
Eat them
Happily.
I'm here
Not in a case
There's no case against me
I'm free
Not in Lebanon

I'm eating falafel, home-made hummus
Without lotsa money.
I'm out of the box,
Playing music,
Singing
Can you hear me?
I'm here.
Goodbye Carlos.

PART THREE

I think it was an *octobass*.
The orchestra's largest instrument:
Octobass.
Three and a half metres tall.
Very rare, hard to play,
Only seven exist.
The seven gods don't move around much.
Hard to carry.
Not hand luggage.

PART FOUR

Under overhanging riverside flood debris
I lie
As far from people and lights as I can be in this blinding
city.
Debris means twigs, branches, reeds and, inexplicably,
many blankets,
Twisted and compacted together artfully by nature.
From below I dwell on that, reflect on that
Awesome power to move
Fixed objects suddenly
From one place to another,
Unbelievably.

Almost miraculously.
Flood power's crushing injustice.
It's very cold.
I'm using my own blanket,
Taking great care to avoid
Comorbid medical conditions.
Many people like me have been swept away
Blankets and all.

PART FIVE

We must force ourselves to believe –
Self-deceive –
That where we are and what we do
Is correct.
[To avoid upset
We may escape in a box.]
Carlos must feel
The bad he's done
Is balanced by the good,
So he set himself up
As judge and deliverer.
He?
I mean 'we',
You
And I.
We say:
Ghosn, gone.
Goodbye Carlos.
But Carlos is with us
Because Carlos is us.

The Past is Like That

Four weeks ago at this spot
I took a photo of
A blazing maple.
Leaves hot red
With the change of autumn,
Set off by a shining sky,
Cloudless and infinite.
Beneath the tree
Were a middle-aged couple
From Nepal –
Unusual for Tokyo.
The man sitting upright and alert
In a multi-coloured cap
And the woman asleep under a shawl.
The man and I shared a few words in basic Hindi,
I took my photo and moved on.
Now today is cold
And I walk alone
Beneath a heavy cloud.
The past is like that –
All the good times we've ever had
Are gone.
I see the leaves are dead and dried on the floor,
The fire burned out of the empty tree.
I walk on,
The wind is cold,
I hope spring will come.

Good Fool

I believe if I act like a good person long enough
Most people can't tell the difference.
So I pretend to be a husband,
A friend,
A positive person.
And sometimes I fool myself.

How We Wrote 'Transit to Eden Bridges'

Taylor Mignon asked me to collaborate with him on a poem and I said: Yes! Taylor suggested we write alternate lines of about 10 words each. He was contacting me by email and didn't know I was by chance visiting England at the time. He was home in Japan.

Taylor started with the first line and we wrote a line a day, responding to the words, sounds or images of the previous line. My lines were influenced by what I was doing and seeing in England. For example, I went to Sunday mass at the church of St Augustine of Hippo. And I walked by dormant rose plants with charming names.

On the tenth day, Saturday 7th March 2020, I was walking along the Southbank of the River Thames, London, when I saw a man seated at a tiny table with a typewriter and a sign, 'Poetry for Sale'. His name was Luke Davis. We chatted, I said, 'Wait two minutes, have to meet two friends.' I came back with my friends and ordered 10 words on the theme 'two people', thinking: me and Taylor, my two friends, me and Luke Davis. Luke typed, I paid all the heaviest coins in my wallet, and told him about the project. Luke said he often wrote with another person, had done so for years.

I didn't tell Taylor about Luke Davis' input until after we'd decided 14 lines was a good place to stop, and I'd created the title. Taylor loved the Luke part.

The photo comes from another poet, Sabine Magnet

TRANSIT TO EDEN BRIDGES

By Taylor Mignon & John Francis Cross

Undercover immig dicks spy on public works digs, then bonus visa...
But I'm suffering a jet-lug and my map's upside down
As Jesus & Mary Chain are just loogin on this plain plane
I pray to Saint Mungo and Saint Augustine of Hippo,
Flaying like a mostly conceived portmanteau,

Smuggling women's toes, skin of rhinos and quickly vicious refreshments,
Snugglewotoes, skirhi & quivirefré & mo' complicated mnemonic devices –
I still don't know who, what or where I am –

Lalaists' made-up paroles more convincing than languages –
Shem & Shaun, Cain & Abel, Tweedledee & Tweedledum, dialectic*
Da eye'n icicle, pee'n peel, bee in Beezlebub, why'n syzygy,
Double blessing, Jack's Wish, Lovely Lady, Precious Time = roses' names.
Suddenly, the language of moonlight butterflies beating their wings
Then my dog feels nostalgic for the Garden of Eden.

*Luke's line

117

Vision

I have a vision of people who are rich in time
Daydreaming
Gorgeous and gigantic projects,
Afloat in their minds
Like underworld continents
And mountainous clouds
In the skies
Of still summer days
Of great expanse
And minimal darkness.
Above is sun, planets and stars,
I see so far
And my eyes have cried the required tears
To make my vision wide and clear.
I see me
And you
Living simply –
Though dressing more colourfully –
Complex in imagination,
With a complexity of calmness
Like forests,
And complexity of sparkling delight
Like coral reefs,
Knowing full well
That being able to give
Is a gift.
Walking,
Meeting
Friends and family,
Society unified by compassion
Not fear.
No nationalism –
Even ironically.

House-proud in the sense
Of wanting to improve the place we are.
I see us being able to *purr*
And doing so,
Sleeping in the sunshine, slipping into warm baths,
Sprinting in joy – if only in our minds,
Alive in love
Some of the time.
Playing music,
If only just fingering
Melodies from human skin,
Touch typing messages,
Crayoning prayers in,
Practical art making
Linking allotments,
E-sport heroes,
And the drawing of animals with coloured pencils,
To café tables and park benches,
Celebrating purposeful achievements in daily
existence,
Knitting networks of energy to warm the hearts of cold
or lonely people,
Making or finding doors
On waste grounds,
Public spaces and
Dead end streets of shame,
Opening windows to a better place,
A vision we can move to.
I see myself there
Aged 88
Collecting pebbles on a shore
Or riverside
For no particular reason more
Than it's pleasant collecting
And might lead to something,

Or just the knowledge that pet rabbits like licking small
stones.
No rabbit will be kept alone.
No dog will be tied.
People who say: *Fish have no feelings*,
Will be slapped in the face.
But I envision no other violence.
No slaves or private cars.
You may eat any animal
You kill yourself
With your own bare hands,
And have prayed to first.
We eat well, have balconies.
Live well, are able to dance and swim.
Every roof is a garden, every garden a tonic.
Everyone has a Bolivian pen pal
Except Bolivians
Who are in charge of Ocean Day celebrations all over
the world.
All religions are respected, practised and shared,
And we all exchange shells
And kisses
At Christmas.
Everyone has friends who are handicapped somehow.
No girl or boy is ever abandoned.
Cocaine is on sale in supermarkets
But we usually choose apples or greens in season.
Opium is provided for tedious train journeys
Of which there are few.
We buy stuff with hugs.
Only super rich people have knife fights,
Live at the Olympics,
You'll get free tickets
If you've had an accident.
I mean you, me, we –

There are no other people,
Because the concept of 'them'
Has no place in my vision.
And everyone is a poet!
Let me be the first one
To share with you today
My vision
And say:
I see you in it.
Now thank you for reading.

A short movie of *Vision* is here: youtu.be/oILavTP7A_o

Thanks

Mika,
Chris, Devanshe, Eiko, Ghiselle, Hiro (hero),
Hiro (poet), Joy, Lawrie, Luke, Karl, Katrina, Mike,
Samm, Sorcha, Sho, Taylor, Tomi

Photo Acknowledgements

Back cover: Ghiselle Camacho
Page 10: Ikenoue Bobtail (Café&Fortune) website
Page 116: Olivetti Dora: Sabine Magnet
All other photos and images: John Francis Cross

Other Works & Links

Drunk God Sees Poet (poems & performances)
I Am Xeluco (novel)
Ghosh in China (novel)
Amazon.com, Amazon Japan, Amazon UK

Fish World
fishworld.bandcamp.com

Johnfranciscross Youtube
Performances, painting, drawing & poem videos
www.youtube.com/channel/UCooWxGBG1-
4bG4JpAhhWuFA

Drunk Poets See God
Facebook: Drunk Poets Tokyo
www.facebook.com/groups/434529363281988/

John Francis Cross

Author of the poetry collection *Drunk God Sees Poet*
and of the novels *Ghosh in China* and *I Am Xeluco*,
John Francis Cross was born in Lancashire,
England, has lived and worked in Galilee, The
Hague, London, Paris, Sydney, Brittany, Hong
Kong, Xiamen, Portsmouth and Chandigarh, and is
now living and writing in Tokyo.
He was Poet-in-Residence at Himalayan Orchard,
August 2019, is the creator of *Fish World* and of
performance/poetry/art videos.
Contact:
johnfranciscross@hotmail.co.uk

Printed in Great Britain
by Amazon

69772636R00078